True Love

Interactive Bible Study

What the Bible says about relationships and marriage

Dr. Chris Richards & Dr. Liz Jones

EP

EP BOOKS (Evangelical Press)
Pistyll Hall, Pistyll, Holywell, UK, CH8 7SH
www.epbooks.org
sales@epbooks.org

EP BOOKS are distributed in the USA by:
JPL Fulfillment
3741 Linden Avenue Southeast,
Grand Rapids, MI 49548.
orders@jpldistribution.com
877 683 6935

First published 2017
British Library Cataloguing in Publication Data available
ISBN: 978-1-78397-201-2

Published by EP Books in association with Lovewise
The two authors are trustees of the charity Lovewise, set up in 2002 to promote Christian teaching about marriage and relationships in schools and church youth groups.
www.lovewise.org.uk

Dr. Chris Richards is a Consultant Paediatrician in Newcastle upon Tyne. He is married and has six children. He is a deacon at Gateshead Presbyterian Church.

Dr. Liz Jones is a retired Community Paediatrician. She is married with three married daughters and nine grandchildren. With her husband, she attends Welbeck Road Evangelical Church, Newcastle upon Tyne.

CONTENTS

INTRODUCTION

It is notable that the Bible begins with a wedding **(Genesis 2:24),** ends with a wedding **(Revelation 19:9)** and Jesus starts his ministry at a wedding **(John 2:1-11)**. This fact reminds us how important marriage and right sexual relationships are to the Lord.

There has been a great change in our culture's attitude to sex and marriage over the last fifty years. Marriage is, sadly, no longer considered to be the only right setting for sexual intimacy and young people are surrounded by sexual temptations. It is in this context that young people desperately need to gain confidence in the Bible and its teaching. This will help them to understand God's will in this area and counter pressure from our society to conform to its ways. To that end, we hope this study is a valuable teaching resource.

The first two studies address the meaning and characteristics of marriage, before the importance of sexual purity is discussed in the three subsequent studies. This emphasis on marriage in the early studies is intentional. Although you may be concerned about the temptations towards wrong sexual behaviour amongst your young people, we consider that young people will not fully understand the importance of sexual purity until they have understood the true nature and importance of the God-given context for sexual intimacy, which is marriage as God designed it.

USING THIS RESOURCE

This leader's handbook has been designed for use in conjunction with the student handbook. We recommend that, if possible, each member of the group has their own copy of the student handbook. This will help them to follow the study and allow them to make notes, some of which may be personal.

The pages of the leader's and student handbooks share the same layout. Questions, discussions and readings will be found on the same page in both handbooks. Suggested answers are only found in the leader's handbook and corresponding space is left in the student handbook for brief notes on each section.

Estimated timings have been allotted to each section to aid with keeping the study moving to its conclusion within a certain duration. The aim is that each study should take between 40 and 60 minutes (though the fifth study may take longer).

It is likely that certain topics will arise from the material covered in this resource that will require longer discussion. In order that the studies keep to time, we suggest that leaders acknowledge and note these topics with a view to discussing them in more detail on a separate occasion. We have included additional content at the end of this leader's handbook to help inform such discussions. It may even be beneficial to consider using this additional material as the basis for further separate studies.

USING THIS STUDY GUIDE

Read. Look up verses in the Bible.

Discussions. Your study leader will help.

Watch the videos. Browse to the URL shown or scan the QR code-block shown. Videos will play in all modern browsers.

Facts and Statistics. These will inform your discussions.

Further study. Optional further reading.

Further discussion. Optional discussions on related topics.

IN THIS STUDY WE AIM TO TEACH

Estimated duration: **40 - 60 minutes.**

1. **There are two states: single and married.**

2. **The Bible assumes that single people are sexually inactive.**

3. **Some remain single to serve God in a special way.**

4. **God created marriage. His design involves the process of leaving parents, cleaving to one another and 'becoming one flesh', in that order.**

5. **Marriage is a public commitment based on vows or promises.**

6. **Co-habitation is wrong, distinct and deficient compared to marriage.**

7. **God's Seventh Commandment is a protection for marriage.**

8. **Marriage promotes family stability.**

1. SINGLENESS AND MARRIAGE

4-6 mins.

Read 1 Corinthians 7:7-9. What do these verses teach us about singleness and marriage (v7)?

They are both gifts from God.

What does the Bible assume about singleness (v9)?

A single person is not sexually active.

8-12 mins.

Is this different from how young people understand singleness in our society?

- *Singleness in society nowadays usually means that the person is not currently in a relationship, whereas Biblical singleness means a person is not married.*
- *In our current society it is considered acceptable for a person who is not married to be sexually active or to cohabit (live together).*
- *There is often the suggestion that a person who is not sexually active is likely to feel unfulfilled.*

Read 1 Corinthians 7:32-35. We all start off single; some remain single for a while, whereas some people remain single for life. What does the Bible say is good about singleness?

That a person can be single-minded about serving God without the responsibility of a wife or husband and children.

Can you think of people who have done jobs or been in situations where being single has enabled them to serve God in a particular way?

The young people may know someone personally who is serving or has served God effectively as a single person. You could mention people such as: Dr. Helen Roseveare, Rev. John Stott, Amy Carmichael or Gladys Aylward.

SEE FURTHER STUDY *(page 45).*

2-4 mins.

Read Genesis 2:18, Genesis 1:27-28, Ephesians 5:31-32. Why did God create marriage?

- *For loving companionship.*
- *To have children.*
- *As a picture of Christ's relationship with the church which is described as His bride.*

2-4 mins.

Read Genesis 2:24. What three aspects of marriage are mentioned in this verse? Note the order.

- *The husband and wife leave their parents.*
- *Unite their lives.*
- *Unite their bodies in sexual intimacy (one aspect of becoming 'one flesh').*

Marriage is a legal commitment based on promises (vows) made in public, usually in front of family and friends at the wedding ceremony.

2-4 mins.

Read Malachi 2:14-16. How does God view the promises (covenant) of marriage?

These verses teach that God views the marriage promises as very important and does not want them to be broken. This is confirmed by what Jesus says in ***Mark 10:6-9****. In the verses that follow Jesus speaks about divorce. It is important to acknowledge to the young people that divorce has sadly become much more common over the last 50 years.*

FURTHER DISCUSSION NOTES ON DIVORCE *(pages 46-48)*

6-9 mins.

VIDEO: THE MARRIAGE VOWS.
http://lovewise.org.uk/true-love-videos/marriage-vows

Listen carefully to the promises this couple make to each other when they get married.

What did the couple getting married promise to each other?

Lifelong faithfulness in all circumstances. This means they will love and look after each other for the rest of their lives until one of them dies, whether they face easy or difficult circumstances, whether they become rich or poor, and whether they are healthy or sick.

5-8 mins.

Cohabitation (living together) means a couple sharing a home and being sexually intimate when they are not married. How is cohabitation different from marriage?

(Be sensitive to the family situations represented in your youth group.)

Possible answers may include:

- *they are going against God's command to keep sexual intimacy for marriage.*
- *they have not made public promises.*
- *they have not signed any legal documents.*
- *they do not have wedding rings.*
- *they do not share a surname.*
- *they would not have to get a divorce if they split up.*
- *they may feel less secure.*
- *they are free to walk away from the relationship; for example, if they find another partner or want to move away because of work etc.*

Cohabiting couples have not made public promises or signed legal documents. Many cohabiting couples have not made a decision about their long term future. Getting married is a decision to make unconditional promises which will radically affect the way a couple views their relationship and how they behave.

The radical difference between cohabitation and marriage is shown by studies demonstrating that cohabiting relationships break up more frequently than marriages – see the study on page 15 for further discussion. Cohabitation unwittingly looks for, or tests for, failure or things that would be each person's "deal breaker". In contrast, marriage involves unconditional love and commitment, and therefore the couple are promising to work through difficulties together.

2-4 mins.

Read Exodus 20:14. How does this commandment relate to marriage?

This commandment protects marriage.

2-4 mins.

What does this graph show about marriage and cohabitation?

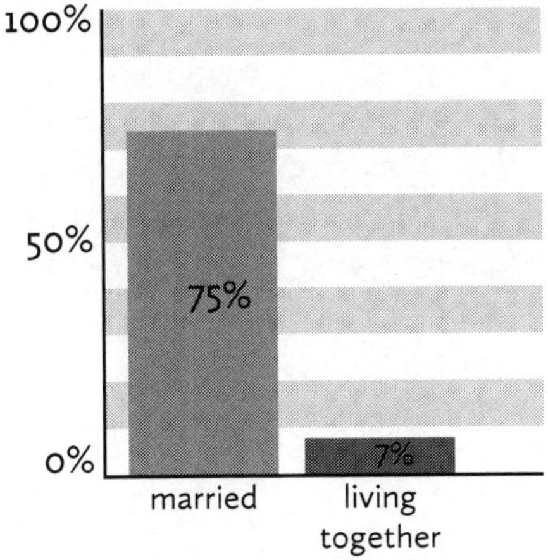

Parents still together when their child reaches 16

From Pronzato C., British Household Panel Survey Consolidated Marital, Cohabitation and Fertility Histories, 1991-2006. 2nd Edition. University of Essex. Institute for Social and Economic Research.

According to this study, by the time a child is 16, if the parents are married, there is a 75% chance that the parents will still be together. If the parents are living together and have never married, there is a 7% chance the parents will still be together. (Some of the married parents will have initially lived together and then got married.)

The graph therefore shows that being married made it more likely that the parents would remain together. The evidence from this study supports the goodness and wisdom of God's design of marriage.

2-4 mins.

Some people say that marriage is "only a piece of paper". Why is marriage more than a piece of paper?

> "*It is not your love that sustains the marriage, but.... the marriage that sustains the love".*

Dietrich Bonhoeffer | German theologian in the Second World War

Love is a feeling and feelings can change, but marriage is a commitment. The fact that a married couple have made legal promises in public and before God sustains the marriage through difficult times when the feelings of love might not be so strong.

IN THIS STUDY WE AIM TO TEACH

Estimated duration: **40 - 60 minutes.**

1. **Marriage is designed by God.**

2. **Marriage is:** Heterosexual.
   Monogamous.
   Lifelong.
   Complementary and unselfish.
   A loving companionship.
   Sexually intimate.
   Faithful.
   Honourable.
   Fruitful.
   A picture of Christ's relationship with the Church.
   Something to be happy about.

3. **Marriage helps children.**

4. **Marriage is under pressure in our society.**

5. **Love has special qualities.**

2. UNDERSTANDING MARRIAGE

What do we learn about marriage from the following verses?

20-30 mins.

Read Matthew 19:4-5.

It is heterosexual, i.e. between a man and his wife, a male and a female.

SEE FURTHER DISCUSSION ***(page 49-53).*** *There have recently been various threats to this God designed pattern for marriage. One of these has been the legalisation of same sex 'marriage'. The other has been the attempted blurring of the distinction between men and women through the promotion of transgender ideology.*

Read 1 Corinthians 7:2.

It is between ***one*** *man and* ***one*** *woman i.e. not polygamous. Monogamy is also affirmed by* ***Genesis 2:24*** *which teaches that two (not more) become one.*

Read Matthew 19:6, Mark 10:7-9.

God intends that a marriage be lifelong because He has united the man and his wife.

Read Ephesians 5:22-29 & 33, Genesis 1:27.

- *It is complementary; a husband and wife are different, but equally valued in the sight of God (because they are both made in God's image).*
- *The husband and wife have different roles which balance and complete each other as they work together.*
- *Both of these roles require loving self-sacrifice.*

SEE FURTHER STUDY ON COMPLEMENTARITY. *(pages 54-58)*

Read Genesis 2:20-23, Proverbs 31:10.

It is a loving companionship. Having found no suitable companion, the first recorded words of Adam reflect his joy when God brings the woman to him.

Read Genesis 2:24, 1 Corinthians 7:2-5.

It is where God designed sexual intimacy to be experienced.

Read Malachi 2:16.

It is intended to be faithful.

Read Hebrews 13:4.

It is to be honoured both from within by the couples themselves, and from outside a marriage by everyone else, including single people.

Read Malachi 2:15.

God desires "godly offspring". One purpose of marriage is to conceive and nurture children in a God-honouring family environment. Statistics show that children born to married parents tend to be healthier both physically and mentally.

(Great care is needed in explaining this as many children are understandably very sensitive if their parents are not married or have divorced.)

Sadly, not all married couples are able to have children. Some adopt and in this way often give a loving stable home to other children.

Read Ephesians 5:30-32.

It is a picture of Christ's relationship with His church which will last for all eternity.

Read Revelation 19:7.

It is something to be happy about, as it reflects the future heavenly joy of the Lamb (Christ) for His bride, the church in the new heaven and the new earth.

6-9 mins.

VIDEO: MARRIAGE AND CHILDREN.
http://lovewise.org.uk/true-love-videos/marriage-children

Discuss what you have learned from the video clip.

- *This couple emphasise that children thrive with the security of knowing that their parents are totally committed to each other regardless of circumstance.*
- *They describe the importance of working together, having different roles and having fun with their children.*
- *They also remember that they will be the role models if their children marry and have their own children in the future.*

5-8 mins.

By marriage a new family unit is formed. Strong families lead to a strong society. What factors put a strain on marriage in our society and how can we guard against them?

Answers might include:

- *lack of money.*
- *losing a job.*
- *not being able to have children.*
- *being unfaithful.*
- *illness or accidents.*
- *having to work away from home.*
- *interfering in-laws.*

Unfaithfulness is the most common cause of marriage break up.

Read 1 Corinthians 13:4-7 and fill out the table below.

10-12 mins.

Love is	**Explain how this aspect of love would be important in a marriage**
Patient	*Not allowing trivial things to harm the relationship*
Kind	*Generous in the way it treats the other person*
Does not envy	*Does not simmer with jealousy*
Does not boast and is not proud	*Not full of bragging and self-importance*
Is not rude	*Behaves well*
Is not self-seeking	*Thinks about the good of the other person (unselfish)*
Is not easily angered	*Does not get irritated or fly into a rage*
Keeps no record of wrong	*Does not hold grudges*
Does not delight in evil but is glad about the truth	*Is loyal to the other person despite their weaknesses and mistakes*
Always protects Always trusts Always hopes Always perseveres Does not fail	*Bears up under difficulties, continues in hope and goes on until one spouse dies.*

IN THIS STUDY WE AIM TO TEACH

Estimated duration: **40 - 60 minutes.**

1. **God designed sexual intimacy for, and only for, marriage.**
2. **We offend God and hurt each other if we are sexually intimate outside marriage.**
3. **There are many positive reasons to keep sex for marriage.**
4. **Sex outside marriage can lead to painful consequences.**

3. WHY KEEP SEX FOR MARRIAGE?

What are the purposes of sexual intimacy?

5-8 mins.

A loving bond for marriage and the way to have children. Note that these are the same as the purposes of marriage – a loving companionship and a secure environment for having and bringing up children. Just as God designed marriage, He also designed sexual intimacy; therefore it has both good and holy purposes.

Discuss how this is different from the way many people in our western culture think about sex.

People think of sex as:

- *recreational.*
- *without consequences.*
- *a private matter in which we can act as we like.*
- *the only way of expressing love.*
- *malleable in terms of gender.*

What do the following parts of the Bible teach us about not keeping sex for marriage?

10-15 mins.

Read Exodus 20:14 and Hebrews 13:4.

It is a sin against God who wants to protect marriage.

Read 1 Corinthians 6:18.

It is a sin against our own bodies. (Mention unintended pregnancy and fatherhood, sexually transmitted infections, emotional problems and regrets.)

Read 1 Corinthians 6:19.

It offends the Holy Spirit who lives in the Christian.

6-9 mins.

VIDEO: MARRYING FOR THE RIGHT REASONS.
http://lovewise.org.uk/true-love-videos/marrying-right-reasons

Listen to this lady's story.

How did sex before marriage affect this lady's marriage relationship? What do we learn from this?

After she had been married to her husband for a short time, she realised that they had not really got to know each other before they married and they had very little in common. They had felt artificially close to each other because they were being sexually intimate. We learn that once sexual intimacy is experienced in a going out relationship, it is more difficult to really get to know each other and assess their suitability as a marriage partner.

6-9 mins.

VIDEO: SAVING SEX FOR MARRIAGE.
http://lovewise.org.uk/true-love-videos/saving-sex-for-marriage

What did these couples say about saving sex for marriage?

- *They said that being sexually active with someone is a big decision that will affect the rest of a person's life.*
- *They thought it was important to talk about saving sex for marriage and to set boundaries in a relationship.*
- *They thought that saving sex for marriage made getting to know each other easier and would benefit their future marriage.*

6-9 mins.

Think of all the positive reasons for keeping sex for marriage.

Suggested answers:

- *it builds up trust and faithfulness in a relationship.*
- *it makes your husband or wife more special.*
- *it makes the wedding, honeymoon and marriage more special.*
- *it means children are born into a loving committed relationship.*
- *it means you do not compare your husband or wife with anyone else so there is no disappointment or jealousy.*
- *it means you do not feel rejection or hurt after you have given your body to someone who then rejects or leaves you.*
- *it means you will not bring a sexually transmitted infection into your marriage.*
- *it pleases God and we reflect God's image to others as we obey and serve Him.*

6-9 mins.

Think of the consequences of sex outside marriage in the lives of the following people in the Bible.

Abraham (**Genesis 16:3-6, Genesis 21:1-9**).

Jealousy and unkindness.

David (**2 Samuel 11:2-17 and 2 Samuel 12:10**).

Deceit, murder and destruction of the family.

Solomon (**1 Kings 11:1-4, 11**).

Backsliding and division of the nation.

IN THIS STUDY WE AIM TO TEACH

Estimated duration: **40 - 60 minutes.**

1. **A Christian should honour God by living in a pure way.**
2. **The purpose of going out is to see if a friendship grows and might lead to marriage.**
3. **It matters who we go out with.**
4. **It matters how we go out.**
5. **Practical advice on keeping sexual intimacy for marriage.**
6. **It is important to keep following the Lord Jesus Christ.**

4. GOING OUT IN A WAY THAT HONOURS GOD

To "honour" in the Bible means to obey and respect (**Exodus 20:12**).

8-12 mins.

Read John 14:23, John 15:5, Matthew 5:8, Hebrews 13:4b and 1 Corinthians 6:20. What do these verses teach us?

If we truly love God, we will obey him. We need to remain close to God to be fruitful in our Christian lives. Purity helps us keep close to God. Doing the right thing will bring blessing in the end, but not following God's ways will bring punishment and sadness in the end. Jesus paid the price of a cruel death by crucifixion and separation from God in order to save us, and, therefore, we should honour him with our bodies.

What is the purpose of "going out"?

2-4 mins.

To get to know the person and see if the friendship grows and might lead to marriage. When a couple start going out, it is important to think carefully about the suitability of the other person as a marriage partner and about the issue of commitment.

It matters <u>who</u> we go out with.

10-15 mins.

Give each member of the group 3 strips of paper and a pen. Ask them to write down 3 things that are essential to them when choosing a girl / boyfriend. Collect up the ideas, go through them together and discuss which of them you think are the most important.

Read 2 Corinthians 6:14 and 1 Corinthians 7:39.
What do these verses teach us?

That a Christian should not enter into a partnership with someone who does not share their love for God and that a Christian should only marry another Christian.

A Christian's first love is God, a Christian's motives are different, their world view is different, their aims and values are different and their ultimate destination is different, when compared to someone who does not love Jesus.

So for a Christian it is also most important that the person you go out with and may later marry is also a Christian.

6-9 mins.

It matters <u>how</u> we go out. While a couple will want to spend time together in order to get to know each other, going out in a way that honours God requires self-control. Self-control is part of the fruit of the Holy Spirit in our lives.

Read 1 Thessalonians 4:1-8.

What do the verses tell us to avoid and why?

- *We must avoid sexual intimacy of all kinds outside marriage, because God wants us to live holy lives and this pleases Him.*
- *This holy living will avoid causing harm to others and avoid God's punishment for sin.*

Read Galatians 5:22.

How does self-control benefit a relationship?

Exercising self-control has many positive outcomes for a relationship. Here are some examples:

- *it shows you respect and care for the other person.*
- *it builds up love and trust in the relationship.*
- *it makes future marriage more special.*
- *it allows you to get to know each other without physical distraction.*
- *it avoids a spiral of greater and greater arousal and intimacy which is hard to resist.*

7-10 mins.

VIDEO: PRACTICAL ADVICE.
http://lovewise.org.uk/true-love-videos/practical-advice

Remembering what you have heard in the video clip and thinking about this for yourself, discuss practical ways which would help a couple keep sexual intimacy for marriage.

You could mention setting boundaries, avoiding alcohol, not being together late at night, keeping clothes on,... there may be other suggestions.

5-8 mins.

Read Hebrews 12:1-3. Discuss what this means for someone who is a Christian. How does Christ's example in these verses help us to follow God's ways in our relationships – even when it seems difficult?

Following God's ways is not always easy especially when what we hear from our friends, in the media or even in lessons at school is totally different from what the Bible teaches. But if we remember Christians from the past, keep looking to Jesus and avoid the situations that might make us do wrong, we can glorify God through our lives. We will also experience the blessing that comes to those who honour Him.

With an eternal perspective, Jesus looked to the future of glory when he went through the terrible suffering and shame of the crucifixion.

IN THIS STUDY WE AIM TO TEACH

Estimated duration: **50 - 75 minutes.**

1. **What temptation is.**
2. **That we can sin sexually without being in a relationship.**
3. **The dangers of pornography & masturbation.**
4. **The unwise use of social media.**
5. **How sexual temptation can affect men & women differently.**
6. **Why certain common ideas are wrong.**
7. **How to deal with sexual temptation.**
8. **About forgiveness and a new start.**

There are four big issues related to this study: pornography, masturbation, same sex attraction and the dangers of social media. Materials for FURTHER DISCUSSION of these issues are found at the end of this book on the *page numbers* indicated. You may want to consider additional studies to tackle these issues separately.

5. SEXUAL TEMPTATION

4-6 mins. **Read James 1:13-15, Matthew 4:1-11 and Joshua 7:19-21.** What is temptation?

- *Temptation is a pull or provocation to sin.*
- *Temptations can come from within us, such as wrong thoughts or fantasies; or from outside us such as what we see or experience.*
- *Temptation works on wrong desires to which, sadly, we are all vulnerable. Satan (the devil) is often the one who tempts us - see **1 Peter 5:8**. But remember temptation itself is not sin; Jesus was tempted, yet was "without sin" **(Hebrews 4:15)**.*

3-5 mins. **Read 1 Corinthians 6:13b and Matthew 5:27-29.** What do these verses teach?

That sexual immorality is using our bodies in a sinful way, including the use of our eyes and minds.

5-7 mins. How is it possible to sin sexually without being in a relationship?

Possible answers include: through our thoughts; through pornography; by masturbation*; through unhelpful books, songs, films, magazines, or games; through unwholesome use of social media.*

***SEE FURTHER DISCUSSION NOTES** *(pages 59-63).*

2-4 mins.

Read Proverbs 12:26 and Proverbs 13:20. What do these verses warn us about?

The Bible warns us to be wise about who we confide in and associate with.

6-9 mins.

Discuss how the use of social media* can become a sexual temptation.

It is easy to get drawn into exchanging internet messages with someone who is not concerned to behave in a God-honouring way and is probably more concerned about themselves than about you.

Sometimes young people are asked to send sexually explicit selfies over the internet. This is both wrong and dangerous. In law such images are 'indecent' and taking, possessing or sharing one (even if it is of yourself) is illegal if the person in the picture is under 18.

*For example, Facebook, Twitter, Youtube, Instagram, Snapchat, MSN, Reddit, computer games or any other platform that contains a comments section, forum or 'chat room' function.

3-5 mins.

Men and women are often vulnerable to sexual temptation in different ways. Can you think what some of the differences might be?

Men are often tempted by things that they see, such as a beautiful woman, a sexually provocative picture or pornography. Some men are also more attracted to sex without commitment.

Women are especially tempted to wrong relationships because of a desire to be loved and the attraction of appreciation and security. When going out, girls may be tempted to yield to pressure to give themselves away sexually in order to secure a relationship.

2-4 mins.

Same sex attraction / activity is an increasing temptation for young people at this time in our culture.

Read Romans 1:18-27. What do these verses teach?

Homosexual activity is sinful and is one of the consequences of people's refusal to honour God in their lives. As an act of judgement, God allows them to follow the sinful desires of their hearts by removing His restraining influence.

SEE FURTHER DISCUSSION *(pages 64-65).*

4 mins.

VIDEO: PRESSURE.
http://lovewise.org.uk/true-love-videos/pressure

This young woman felt pressurised to be sexually intimate with her boyfriend in order to secure the relationship. Sadly this did not happen and their relationship ended.

8-12 mins.

It is not wrong to find someone attractive, to want to get married, or to go out to see if future marriage is even a possibility; but in any of these circumstances it is possible to be tempted to sin.

On the next page, read the three statements, look up the Bible references and discuss why each statement is wrong:

" It is culturally acceptable to be sexually active before or outside marriage, especially if contraception is used.

Read Hebrews 13:4, Hebrews 11:25.

We should keep pure for future marriage and faithful when married. The Bible teaches that though sin may be enjoyable for a while, the enjoyment fades and longer term pain and damage often set in.

" We can do whatever feels good.

Read Titus 2:6, Galatians 5:22, 2 Peter 1:5-9 and 1 Peter 3:3-4.

Self-control is a fruit of the Holy Spirit in the lives of all true Christians. Young men, particularly, are encouraged to have self-control. Young women are encouraged to think about the inner qualities of gentleness, purity and godliness.

" Being in a relationship is the most important thing in my life.

Read Exodus 20:3.

It is possible that the idea of going out, or the person we are going out with, becomes more important to us than honouring God and so becomes an idol.

2-3 mins.

Read Psalm 119:9-11. How could you guard against the temptations we have discussed?

By reading and knowing God's word.

2-3 mins.

Read Genesis 39:12. How did Joseph deal with sexual temptation?

By running away.

2-3 mins.

Read James 4:7-8a. What should we do when Satan tempts us?

Say "no", submit to God's will, draw near to Him through prayer and entrust your life to Him.

6 mins.

If we feel guilty about some form of sexual sin, it is important to ask God for forgiveness and strength to turn away from sin.

Read 1 John 1:9.

Some of the young people in the group may have already sinned in this area and need to confess their sin to God. Explain that God is able and willing to forgive those who are genuinely sorry for their sin, because Jesus took the punishment we deserve through His death on the cross. Through the death and resurrection of Jesus we can be sure that there is always a new start for those who truly repent and trust in Him.

VIDEO: A NEW START.
http://lovewise.org.uk/true-love-videos/new-start

3-4 mins.

The same young woman we have already seen in the last video, later became a Christian, knew forgiveness and then approached relationships in a completely different way.

FURTHER STUDY TOPICS

This section includes notes and suggested further study resources on topics that have been raised during the studies and may need further discussion. It is hoped that these notes and the suggested further study resources will help the leader to clarify and enable the young people to understand the Biblical teaching relevant to these issues.

Topics covered:

SINGLE MINISTRY BIOGRAPHIES

FURTHER STUDY

The following resources may be useful:

- Iain H. Murray **'Amy Carmichael: Beauty for Ashes - A Biography'**, *The Banner of Truth Trust, April 2015.*
- Dr. Helen Roseveare **'Give Me This Mountain'**, *Christian Focus, January 2012.*
- Chris Wright **'John Stott. A Portrait by His Friends'**, *IVP, 2011.*
- Gladys Aylward with Christine Hunter **'Gladys Aylward: The Little Woman'**, *Moody Press, June 1970.*

DIVORCE

ISSUES RAISED

For young people growing up, divorce is a very sensitive topic and, sadly, one which many of them will have had to face and live with in their own families. More than one in four children are now likely to see their parents divorced before they reach the age of sixteen. Divorce is so commonplace that many young people may think of it as almost normal. It may be seen as the justified way out of a difficult marriage. It may even encourage young people to accept a less than wise match for a marriage partner, thinking that there is always a way of escape if things do not go well.

BIBLICAL PERSPECTIVE

The Bible records the Pharisees asking Jesus **(Matthew 19:3)** whether it was acceptable for a man to divorce his wife for any and every reason. Jesus went back to creation and reminded His hearers of God's original design of marriage recorded in **Genesis 2:24**. He stated that marriage was intended to be permanent (as long as husband and wife both remained alive), saying "what God has joined together, let man not separate" **(Matthew 19:6 and Mark 10:9)**. Jesus also said that when Moses permitted divorce **(Deuteronomy 24:1-4)**, it was only "because of the hardness of your hearts", i.e. a gracious concession in a sinful world, and was intended to emphasise the permanence of separation in a situation where the woman was vulnerable due to desertion. Some Christians interpret Jesus's comment "except for sexual immorality" **(Matthew 19:10)**, as permitting divorce in the limited circumstances of adultery or desertion.

The prophet **Malachi (Chapter 2)** reminds his hearers of their moral accountability in marriage as created beings before God **(v10)**. He calls marriage a covenant (a relationship based on promises) **(v14)** with the purpose of producing godly offspring **(v15)** and reminds "that God hates divorce" **(v16)**. Paul spoke about the holiness of marriage when he explained it was a picture of the relationship between Christ and the church **(Ephesians 5:32)**. Marriage is rightly called 'holy matrimony' and it is to be held in reverence by a married couple. In taking the marriage vows, a couple promise before God to be faithful to one another whatever the circumstances "til death us do part". It is important to encourage young people to see the seriousness of a vow before God and the implications for the permanence of marriage.

LEGAL SITUATION IN THE UK

Divorce was only legalised in 1857 and allowed when a spouse had committed adultery. The grounds for divorce were widened in 1937 to include desertion, cruelty, and incurable insanity. The 1969 Divorce Reform Act made it possible to obtain a divorce on the grounds of a two year separation if both partners agreed and a five year separation if only one partner agreed. This was called 'no fault' divorce. Since 1969 the number of divorces occurring in England and Wales has increased significantly and there are people lobbying parliament to make a divorce still easier to obtain.

PRACTICAL APPLICATION

While there are undoubtedly cases where divorce has made it possible for a partner to leave an abusive situation, in general, easier divorce has made marriage less secure. Divorce seems to offer an easier and quicker route than putting in the work required to resolve difficult issues and work towards the healing of relationships.

Over the last fifty years marriage has increasingly been seen as an institution which is primarily about the satisfaction of the two people involved rather than their children. This perspective has served to increase divorce. Many thought that divorce would lessen the conflict between parents, but in many cases it has actually caused it to increase.

FURTHER STUDY

The following resources may be useful:

- The Christian Institute 'Divorce search', **http://www.christian.org.uk/?s=divorce** *The Christian Institute, 2017.*
- Jay E. Adams **'Marriage, Divorce, And Remarriage In The Bible',** *Zondervan, 1986.*
- Gordon J. Wenham, William A. Heth, Craig S. Keener **'Remarriage After Divorce – Three Views in Today's Church',** *Zondervan, 2006.*

THE LEGAL 'REDEFINITION' OF MARRIAGE

ISSUES RAISED

Young people may raise the issue that since 2013 it has been legal in England and Wales for same sex couples to marry. Some may see this as fair for those who are attracted to the same sex.

HISTORICAL AND BIBLICAL BACKGROUND

Until recently, in law, in society and in culture marriage was understood as:

> *the voluntary union for life of one man and one woman to the exclusion of all others.*
>
> *Lord Penzance in Hyde v. Hyde (1866)*

Marriage was designed by God. The first man and woman created by God, Adam and Eve, were also husband and wife. This set a pattern for men and women to follow in the future. **Genesis 2:24 (NIV)** describes the basic design of marriage: "a man will leave his father and mother and be united to his wife, and they will become one flesh". Marriage has been present since the creation of the world and is therefore known as a 'creation ordinance'. Marriage is recorded throughout history and in all nations around the world, even by people who would not necessarily recognise God as its designer.

From the beginning of history marriage has brought a man and a woman together; this joining of the two sexes is called a complementary union. A man and woman are different not only in their bodies, but also in their thoughts and feelings. These differences allow them to take on different roles in marriage, and to work together in a complementary way that benefits each other and their new family (social) unit.

One of God's purposes for marriage is procreation and it is only through the sexual union of a man and a woman that new life is naturally conceived. Thus marriage not only brings two people together, but it often involves the conceiving and raising of children in a family. Historically, marriage has involved a public understanding that the couple will remain sexually faithful to each other and stay together for life, enabling children to be raised in a stable environment. The married family is a powerful God-given structure that impacts and strengthens wider communities and society as a whole.

Over the last fifty years many in society have rejected the married family as natural, and promoted the idea that 'family' can be any group of people who live together or care for each other, and can be constructed as we want. In Western culture gender distinctions have been challenged and society is now marked by individualism and autonomy*. This means that personal freedom and fulfilment has become paramount, so we should not feel any obligation to remain in a situation which is difficult or imperfect. Furthermore, the argument follows,

---

* *Individualism is a social theory favouring the free action of individuals. Autonomy means acting independently or having the freedom to do so. These ideas are the result of a long process of change in thinking which goes back nearly three centuries to a time when philosophers began to suggest that human reason was more important than the truth God has revealed to us in the Bible. Over time, this has resulted in the current idea that, in general, we all have the right to believe and do what we want.*

if marriage is all about individual fulfilment, then same sex couples should not be denied the right to marry. This so-called 'marriage' then ceases to have anything to do with a person's biological sex **(Genesis 1:26,27)**, and therefore their ability to naturally conceive a child. It also no longer reflects God's design in which husband and wife complement each other **(Genesis 2:24)**. Since God's definition of marriage is the only true one and cannot be altered, this is not true marriage, though it may be legally recognised. The outworking of this change is likely to cause much damage and confusion.

In July 2013, the Westminster Parliament passed legislation to permit same-sex couples to marry in England and Wales.

FURTHER STUDY

The following resources may be useful:

- Sharon James **'The Meaning of Marriage – How the sexual revolution has changed our understanding of society's basic building block'**, *Family Education Trust, 2013.*
- The Christian Institute **'Redefining marriage – Same sex marriage and its consequences'**, *The Christian Institute, 2012.*

TRANSGENDER

ISSUES RAISED

Transgender is a broad term for those who feel they are in the wrong body. Historically a person's gender was the same as their biological sex. Lately your gender is considered to be what you think you are and this may not be consistent with your biological sex. In 2004, the Gender Recognition Act enabled adults who were dissatisfied with their born gender to apply for legal recognition of their 'new gender' and to obtain a Gender Recognition Certificate. There are now numerous different options for classifying a person's gender. So, in law, gender identity is now considered superior to biological sex. In other words perceptions have become the reference point rather than the body as God made it.

Some adults with gender confusion or gender dysphoria have chosen to undergo so-called gender reassignment surgery and now children who feel they are in the wrong body are encouraged to embrace these feelings and may receive hormone blocking treatment in anticipation of gender reassignment surgery later. The protection of personal autonomy means some people see these changes as totally justified.

Very rarely infants are born with an intersex condition, where disease due to chromosomal or anatomical abnormality causes ambiguity of gender. Such conditions have been used by those who want to prove the existence of a gender spectrum. However, they bear witness to an opposite truth. Both parents and doctors seek to identify the true, or when uncertain, most likely, gender and, if possible provide medical interventions to help the child to develop and function as normally as possible in that gender. This is not always easy or successful, but neither parent nor doctor usually seeks to promote gender ambiguity, giving witness to the binary nature of gender.

BIBLICAL PERSPECTIVE

At creation "God created man in His own image; in the image of God He created him; male and female He created them" **(Genesis 1:27)**. Our biological sex is, therefore, given to us by God. It is part of our essence, just as is being made in God's image. It permeates our minds, bodies and spirit and is part of our identity. Though people may be raised in difficult family environments and be encouraged or provoked to be discontented or confused about who they are and what sex they feel they are, no-one ought to try to be something that they are not. Attempting to change one's sex is wrong and is an actual impossibility. The result is a lie, and demands that others confirm the lie. There are testimonies of those who have undergone an attempt at sex change that indicate a lack of fulfilment of their hopes. Such people need help to realise and appreciate their God-given sex.

FURTHER STUDY

The following resources may be useful:

- Sharon James **'http://www.affinity.org.uk/downloads/The%20Bulletin/32.1)-are-we-all-omnigender-now.pdf'**, *Affinity, 2016.*
- R. Albert Mohler, Jr. **'We Cannot Be Silent', Chapter 5**, *Nelson Books, 2015.*

COMPLEMENTARITY

BACKGROUND

The husband and wife are both created in the image of God and are, therefore, equal in dignity ("heirs together of the grace of life" – **1 Peter 3:7**). However, just as their bodies and minds are different, so too are their roles. The husband and wife are what is termed 'complementary' to each other. 'Complementarity' can be defined as the working together of different roles and abilities for the good of both parties. A husband and wife complement each other so as to make the marriage whole. This allows the marriage to work as God intended.

AN EXERCISE ON COMPLEMENTARITY (also in the student handbook)

Part 1 – Look up the following passages and think how they describe the distinctive roles of husband and wife.

Husband		Wife	
Eph 5:23-29 & 33	*Headship involving loving leadership*	**Eph 5:22-24 & 33, Col 3:18**	*Submission, respect*
1 Pet 3:7	*Protection, honour/respect*	**Gen 2:18-24**	*Help, support*
Gen 3:17 & 19, 2 Thess 3:10	*Breadwinner*	**Titus 2:5, Prov 31:10-31**	*Homemaker*
Eph 6:4, Col 3:21	*Fatherhood*	**Titus 2:4**	*Motherhood*

Part 2 – In the light of these distinctive roles, list some of the qualities which you and others might seek to develop, in order to prepare for such roles. Note that these are important qualities to develop, whether you get married or not.

Boys	Girls	Both
Honour/respect, purity towards women	*Modesty* ***(1 Tim 2 9-15)****; inward beauty* ***(Prov 31:30)***	*Love* ***(I Cor 13)*** *Wisdom* ***(Prov 1:7)***
Taking initiative – including in Bible study/prayer ***(1 Tim 2:8)***	*Kindness (for poor,* ***Prov 31:20;*** *for children & husband,* ***Titus 2:4-5****)*	*Patience and understanding with/of other sex* ***(1 Pet 3:7)***
Responsibility (sober-minded, self-controlled) ***(Titus 2:6)***	*Diligence* ***(Prov 31:13,15)***	*Knowledge of and faithfulness to God's word*
Hard work	*Homemaking skills (cooking, cleaning, childcare)*	
Practical skills including DIY!		

A NOTE ON SOME ROLES AND QUALITIES

Here is a more detailed discussion of the qualities of ***modesty*** and ***honour*** and the roles of ***headship*** and ***submission***.

MODESTY (1 Timothy 2:9-11) is the moral characteristic in which a woman avoids being sexually provocative and does not make a show of her sexual attributes, aware that this pleases God.

A modest attitude will be reflected in the way that a woman dresses, talks and behaves, so that sexual provocation is avoided, remembering that Christians are united as members of Christ's body and that we need to consider the interests of others as well as ourselves **(Phil 2:4)**. This requires careful and wise thought since this should not compromise a woman's God-given desire to look feminine and attractive, and to keep her body healthy. However, rather than focus all her energies on outward appearance, she is to concentrate on seeking the beauty "of the hidden person of the heart, the incorruptible beauty of a gentle and quiet spirit, which is very precious in the sight of God" **(1 Peter 3:4)**.

HONOUR (1 Peter 3:7) is the moral attitude of a man which compels him to treat a woman with respect as the weaker sex. He should recognise her greater vulnerability to emotional manipulation by men **(see Genesis 3:16)** and, in most situations, her lesser physical strength. However, at the same time, the man must also learn to respect her views and insights. Showing honour requires careful consideration. It can seem hard to do amidst the attitude of our current society.

HEADSHIP (Ephesians 5:23) is the position of authority appointed by God, which is given to the husband over his wife and children. We note from this passage that the husband is not commanded to be head – he is head. A husband, therefore, cannot avoid being head – we cannot ask whether he is the head but, before God, we may ask whether he performs the responsibilities of this role faithfully or not.

He puts the role of headship into practice by his leadership of, provision for **(2 Thessalonians 3:10)** and protection of **(1 Peter**

3:7) his family. He takes responsibility for his wife and children's spiritual, material and emotional wellbeing. Leadership involves taking the initiative and taking the responsibility for the consequences of his decisions. He must make the final decisions as 'the buck stops with him'. How this works out in practice will vary according to family circumstances, but, for example, often a husband's job will dictate the family's location. Following the example of Christ, this leadership needs to be loving, servant-like and sacrificial. The husband will be aware of his dependence on the Lord for all wisdom and strength.

How are the skills of leadership developed? They may be role modelled by one's parents **(Proverbs 1:8-10)**. In a godly household the importance of authority is felt, discipline is applied and responsibility developed **(Titus 2:6)**. Others may need to find role models in godly leaders in the church. Taking positions of responsibility at school and later at work, will also help to develop a man's leadership skills.

SUBMISSION (Ephesians 5:22) for a wife is the act of acknowledging and being willing to sit under the God-given authority of her husband. She puts this role into practice by encouraging (and not discouraging) her husband in his leadership responsibilities. She also assists him as his helper **(Genesis 2:18-24)** particularly in providing for and protecting the family. We can see this illustrated clearly in the portrait of a 'virtuous wife' in **Proverbs 31:10-31**.

A woman is required to submit in a special way to the God-given authority of her husband, as to no other man. She can be best prepared for this by learning to have a submissive attitude towards the authority of her parents, especially, where possible, a godly father.

But we must remember that both men and women are called to submit lovingly to one another in a more general way **(Ephesians 5:21)**. All of us need to learn to "esteem others better than ourselves" and to consider the "interests of others" as well as our own **(Philippians 2:3-4)**.

FURTHER STUDY

The following resources may also be helpful:

- Owen Strachan, Gavin Peacock **'The Grand Design: Male and Female He Made Them',** *Christian Focus, 2016.*
- Carrie Sandom **'Different by Design: God's Blueprint for Men and Women',** *Christian Focus, 2013. (*Especially helpful for female readership.)

PORNOGRAPHY

ISSUES RAISED

Some may not consider the use of pornography to be sexual sin, because it does not involve physical sexual intimacy. Some may see the use of pornography as an acceptable means of damage limitation for sexually starved individuals.

BIBLICAL PERSPECTIVE

Matthew 5:27-29 teaches that we can sin sexually with our eyes and minds. It is, therefore, possible to sin sexually without being in a relationship. The use of pornography is such a sin. Though 'heart adultery', as Jesus describes it in **(v28)**, may be a lesser sin than adultery, it is never right to knowingly and deliberately sin against God. Jesus highlights the seriousness of such sins **(v29)** by emphasising that it is worth taking radical steps to avoid their awful eternal consequences. Many who use pornography can testify to a strong sense of guilt and shame associated with its use, reminding us that its use goes against God's law written on our hearts **(Romans 2:15)**.

UNWELCOME CONSEQUENCES

Rather than releasing or easing sexual desire, the use of pornography, often used together with masturbation, inflames such desires and makes it harder for them to be contained outside of marriage. Someone has likened it to putting a cake into a hot oven and expecting it not to burn.

As with all sinful acts, the use of pornography has unwelcome consequences. Its use damages our relationship with God. As with all deliberate sin, it displeases God **(2 Samuel 11:27b)** and threatens the working of His Holy Spirit within us **(1 Corinthians 6:19)**. It also damages our relationships with other people. Its use warps our understanding of the loving basis of the marriage relationship by separating sexual acts from a relationship. It makes it harder to form a good relationship and can ruin a current or future marriage. It encourages us to think of people as objects and can affect the way we treat people as well as give us unrealistic expectations of how people should look and act. It will leave lasting images in the mind, can make people self-absorbed and reclusive, and its use can even become addictive. The people engaged in the pornography industry are often exploited and abused and the industry is closely linked to trafficking and prostitution.

PRACTICAL ADVICE

God's word protects against sinning **(Psalm 119:9-11)**, so get to know relevant verses quoted in this study. Pray for God's strength to overcome temptation **(Matthew 26:41)** and meet regularly with your church family **(Hebrews 10:24-25)**. It is important to take practical steps to stay away from pornography through being careful about what you are shown and what you decide to watch and read. Turn on safe search and use appropriate filters.

If you have made mistakes, God offers forgiveness and a new start **(1 John 1:9)**. Talk to someone you trust, repent, avoid situations which might lead you to sin again and keep going **(Hebrews 4:15-16)**. In the future remain accountable to the person you have already spoken to about your difficulties.

FURTHER STUDY

The following Lovewise resources may be helpful on the issue of pornography (**lovewise.org.uk**):

- **'Staying Pure Online'** – for church youth groups and Christian families'.
- **'Pornography Dangers and Decisions'** – for use in schools.

The following resource may also be helpful:

- Tim Chester **'Captured by a Better Vision'**, *Inter-varsity Press, 2010.*

MASTURBATION

ISSUES RAISED

This is a common topic of concern (as well as embarrassment) for young people. Some may see it as a legitimate way out of sexual frustration.

For some it may be important to deal with this subject, but for others it could cause a breaking of innocence or temptation to impurity. It is important that leaders consider carefully the wisdom of mentioning this topic.

BIBLICAL PERSPECTIVE

Though the Bible does not directly refer to masturbation, we should apply the biblical principle that all deliberate sexual arousal (including self-arousal) caused by lustful thoughts and actions outside marriage is wrong **(see Matthew 5:28 and Galatians 5:19)**. Masturbation separates a sexual act from a relationship, whereas God plans sexual activity to take place within the relationship of marriage.

We should not ignore our conscience's witness. As with pornography, many can testify to a strong sense of guilt and shame associated with its use. As with pornography, rather than releasing or easing sexual desire, masturbation often inflames such desires and makes it harder for them to be contained outside of marriage.

With this as well as other temptations God promises His strength and help:

> “*No temptation has overtaken you that is not common to man. God is faithful, and he will not let you be tempted beyond your ability, but with the temptation he will also provide the way of escape, that you may be able to endure it.*
>
> **1 Corinthians 10:13**

HOMOSEXUALITY

ISSUES RAISED

Some young people may have themselves or know of others who have experienced attraction to people of the same sex and may be concerned to know whether it is permissible to express this attraction in homosexual activity. They may even see it as an individual's right to express their sexuality as they wish. This view is often held up by the error of an autonomous perspective mentioned at the end of the further study notes on the legal 'redefinition' of marriage.

BIBLICAL PERSPECTIVE

1 Corinthians 6:9-11 and **1 Timothy 1:10** make it clear that homosexual activity is wrong. Biologically and physically it goes against the way God created people to act.

Romans 1:18-32 teaches that homosexual desire is against God's created order. The passage explains that an individual's rejection of God is followed by removal of His restraining influence which in turn leads to lustful desires that are against nature (unnatural). Homosexual and lesbian practices are specifically mentioned.

PRACTICAL IMPLICATIONS

Homosexual desires may occur during puberty as part of the process of maturing sexually and pass; in some cases they may remain or develop. Whether they are transient or enduring, it is important to understand homosexual attraction as a temptation to sin (in a similar way to the attraction of a married man towards someone who is not his wife is a temptation to adultery). It is important for single people to realise that they are able to live full lives without needing to express their sexual desires, just as Jesus led a perfectly pure and obedient life on earth without any sexual relationship.

Those who experience same sex attraction need to ask the Lord for help to "lead them not into temptation". The Christian will need to put such desires to death in order that they might be "alive to God in Christ Jesus" **(Romans 6:11)**.

FURTHER STUDY & SUPPORT

For further explanation of passages in the Bible which mention homosexuality, see:

- Sam Alberry **'What does the Bible say about homosexuality'**, *on the Living Out website/questions.*
- Kevin DeYoung **'What Does the Bible Really Teach about Homosexuality?'**, *Crossway, 2015.*

Christian organisations that support people with concerns about same sex attraction include:

- The True Freedom Trust, **truefreedomtrust.co.uk**
- Living out, **www.livingout.org**

TRUE LOVE BOOK

A helpful companion piece or follow up to this Bible study, or to be read as a stand-alone resource – this book has also been written by Dr. Chris Richards and Dr. Liz Jones for Lovewise. It gives useful answers with real life examples and practical applications – all within a Biblical framework.

'It takes courage to write a book about God's standards on relationships and sex, and it will take courage to read it. But the authors have dared to be honest, spelling out the joys and responsibilities of living as God intended. To take this on board will save many tears and heartaches, bringing fulfilment and pleasure in their place. This is a book for everyone to read.'

Roger Carswell

Lovewise is a charity set up in 2002 which is committed to teaching young people about God's design for marriage, relationships, and sex. Lovewise produce a range of resources for both teenagers and pre-teens for use by parents, in church youth groups and in schools.

www.lovewise.org.uk